MW01065841

SAINT
ALBERTUS
MAGNUS

The Secret of Saint Albert's
Consecration of Himself to God

The Secret of Saint Albert's
Dedication of Himself to Man

Done into English and Edited
by
SAINT ALBERTUS COLLEGE

SAINT CATHERINE'S PRESS
Racine, Wisconsin

1938

NIHIL OBSTAT:

H. B. RIES
Censor librorum

IMPRIMATUR:

✠ SAMUEL A. STRITCH
Archiepiscopus Milwaukiensis
February 2, 1938

ALBERTUS MAGNUS, BISHOP OF RATISBON

CONTENTS

Foreword

> *"He is truly zealous for souls who by holy contemplation and fervent desire, by tears and prayers, by night-watchings and fasts, by preaching and the hearing of confessions, by wise counsel, salutary correction, and other good works labors for the salvation of souls."*
> —*Saint Albertus Magnus.*

A better and more concise characterization of Saint Albert is hardly possible than that which he himself has given us in the words quoted above. The following essays are an attempt on the part of his Brethren to give a more detailed presentation of the traits of the Saint.

May the reader, through a more intimate knowledge of the great Saint and Doctor of the Church, ever become more devoted and more faithful in imitating him.

Maurus M. Niehues, O.P.

I
The Secret of Saint Albert's Consecration of Himself to God

Albertus Magnus and Our Own Times
By Maurus M. Niehues, O.P., S.T.L.

"All things have their season, and in their times all things pass under heaven" (*Eccles. iii. 1*).

WE MAY appropriately apply this quotation from Holy Scripture to the canonization of Blessed Albert. More than six and a half centuries had elapsed since his death, and his devout clients had seemingly prayed in vain for his canonization. But finally their trustful prayer was answered, for Albertus Magnus stands before us today a Saint and a Universal Doctor of the Church. This two-fold dignity bestowed on Blessed Albert in our own day, may be considered a dispensation of Divine Providence effecting a renascence which is not yet fully comprehended. Thus the canonization has its season, and has a great purpose to fulfill in our own day.

The well-known Mateo Crawley, a world-apostle in the truest sense of the word, who proposed to himself to gain all men for the Heart of Jesus and who labored with marked success in every land, summed up his wide experience in these words: "Society is so sorely afflicted because it has lost all sense of the Divine." A sad truth which we find confirmed day by day in the lives of innumerable human beings and in so many momentous happenings throughout the world! Society has become positively godless and irreligious. During the past, science, estranged from God, robbed society of its taste for the supernatural; moreover, a purely worldly culture with its highly developed technique and its claims to the practical wisdom of life directed men's thoughts ever more and more to mundane things.

There necessarily resulted a submersion into the material and a gradual tendency toward the purely natural. The awful World War with its aftermath of evils, difficulties,

3

and disturbances everywhere hastened the crisis. The decisive day came, a day that would determine the fate, not of one people only, but of all the world. What would the issue be? A tendency toward God, or a turning away from Him? Recognition of a divine order in the world, or of bolshevistic disorder? Humble faith in God, or a radical denial of God? A consecration of our lives to God, or a total separation from Him? A choice had to be made. At this critical point occurs the canonization of Albertus Magnus. His life affords the world a touchstone for the testing of the spirits. A great man is needed, and Divine Providence supplies him—a man whose endeavor throughout a long life was to snatch souls from the paths of sin and direct them along the lofty ways of holiness.

In the bull of canonization, Pius XI ascribes to Albert the wisdom of Solomon which, while it intimately unites the soul in holiness with God and far surpasses all goods of this earth, fills even more bountifully the hearts of the faithful and attracts them mightily.

Few saints of the Middle Ages are destined so providentially as Saint Albert to fulfill the needs of our age and to bring about its renewal. By his marvelous fund of knowledge he renders the same service to present day society as he rendered to society in the thirteenth century. But as a saint of God he offers us more; namely, a model worthy of imitation. We who have consecrated our lives to God will do well to choose Saint Albert as our ideal and leader to direct us "unto the knowledge of the mystery of God" (Coll. ii. 3), "instructing us that, denying ungodliness and worldly desires, we should live soberly and justly and godly in this world" (Titus ii. 12).

Saint Albert's great purpose in life, as we have seen, was to lead men to God. To attain this end he consecrated himself to God. It is both interesting and instructive to trace the course of his consecration and to note the blessings flowing from it upon himself and upon all his endeavors.

4

Albert was born in 1193 at Lauingen in Germany in the ancestral castle of the noble Bollstädt family, and there he passed the days of his childhood. A careful religious training under the parental roof marks the first step in the preparation for his life's work. Nurtured by the dew of heavenly grace, the heart of the innocent child expanded and took pleasure in God and in all that pertains to God. This joy is a characteristic trait in our Saint, and all through life it quickened his steps along the paths of duty. He experienced this joy particularly in his study of the Psalms and in the attendance at divine services; in the contemplation of the beauties of nature and in the study of her laws; but above all in the contemplation of God and His infinite perfections. The more his heart experienced joy, the more he realized that all true joy is fundamentally sympathetic, that no human being is sufficient unto himself. This conviction drew him all the closer to God, the Author of all good, and caused the first ray of the Dominican *Soli Deo*— God alone—to enter his youthful soul.

About this time the saintly and zealous Dominican, Jordan of Saxony, addressed the students of the University of Padua on the mission of the newly-founded Order of Preachers. His words so deeply impressed Albert that he resolved to quit the world and to dedicate himself to God forever. At the age of thirty, matured by prayer and study and urged on by the grace of God, he carried out his resolution and entered the Order of St. Dominic. He received the white habit from the hands of Blessed Jordan and soon afterwards made his religious profession. This latter was an act of unreserved consecration to the fulfillment of which he henceforth devoted his life. He consecrated himself to God by charity; to truth by study and teaching; to souls by apostolic labors. In this threefold dedication the God-like Albert spent himself in the service of his Maker and taught us in what manner a world estranged from God may be led back to Him.

The World of Nature Leads Albertus Magnus to God

By Eberhard M. Welty, O.P., Ph.D., S.T.L.

MEN AND WOMEN of our day, even practical Catholics, have at times a peculiar notion about sanctity. A saint, so they believe, belongs in a medieval setting. They conceive him to be a person in whom human nature is dulled and distorted by a gloomy and melancholy existence from which every friendly ray of sunlight is banished. Our times are unfavorable to an interior life—a life spent in recollection with God. Men do not aspire to holiness of life; they do not labor earnestly to attain it; they offer the excuse that holiness requires efforts beyond human strength and that the means to gain holiness are unsuitable to this age. They argue that to arrive at sanctity one must refrain from living according to nature; that one must refuse to be interested in scientific attainments and cultural progress; that, in general, an age of refinement, love of nature, and systematic labor does not lend itself to the acquisition of virtue and holiness.

We wish to disprove this erroneous and strange idea of the modern world by offering for study the life of Albertus Magnus, a saint in whom grace and nature were harmoniously united. Saint Albert sought God and found Him in the great expanse of nature, in the ceaseless and assiduous activities of life, in the assertion and development of a sound and noble manhood. Our times are notable for an influx of life from the country into the cities; this influx bears a direct relation to our rapidly increasing industries. The cities, moreover, offer or seem to offer better opportunities for development and progress. Within the last years, however, a counter movement has manifested itself to advantage. Men are again attracted by the beauties of nature; they are lured from the crowded tenements and congested streets into the open country, into the bright sunlight and the wide expanse of the heavens where, far removed from the din and bustle of city traffic, the senses are refreshed by the luxurious plant life; and the body, invigorated by a pure atmosphere and wholesome food.

Saint Albert loved nature as few men have loved it. In early childhood he was accustomed to stand and gaze with wonder at the beauties of nature about him. What delight it gave him to muse on the fishes in merry play near the surface of the water, to join his friends in excursions into the country, or to accept an invitation to a hawking party. When in later years Saint Albert engaged in writing his standard works, he became deeply engrossed in the mysteries of nature, and he treated his subject with an accuracy, a clearness, and holy respect that betoken the reverence he entertained for the wonders of creation.

Love of nature is no obstacle to piety or to the fear of God. All nature proclaims the existence of God, and God converses with man through the medium of nature. His hand fashions and blesses all His creation. In this light Saint Albert contemplated nature. All life and activity seemed to him a splendid reflection of the life of God; a participation in the magnificent and bountiful goodness and benevolence of the Creator, a ray beaming forth from the Deity flooded in light. He beheld traces of the Divine Spirit, of the beauty and majesty of God in every creature. But his duties and responsibilities all through life were so numerous and manifold that only at rare intervals could he enjoy close contact with nature.

Our age delights in boasting of its economic successes, its mastery of technique, and its productiveness through human exertion. This progress we are told is due to the concentration of our interests on the material instead of on the spiritual as was common in medieval times. Men in that age, we are told, hovered in regions far above the earth and held themselves aloof from its affairs, thus re-tarding rather than advancing civilization. The eminently useful life of the Saint proves this reasoning totally false. Grace is not detrimental to natural endowments, neither does it disincline man to noble exertion nor destroy the joy of creating.

Saint Albert made definite contributions to culture. Strange as it may seem, he even ventured into the realm of mechanics. What astonishes us most, however, is that the burden of his duties and the wide range of his activities never made him lose sight of God; they rather became the means of his closer union with Him. He consecrated his work to God, and for that reason it was productive of so much good. The nervous, feverish haste of our age was unknown to the Saint. It was only the love of God that urged him to labor and to fulfill the obligations of his call-ing. He did not cease to pray while at work; and, when he prolonged the time of prayer, it was to draw the blessing of heaven more abundantly upon his labor and to make it fruitful with the dew of grace. To employ all his faculties in the service of God so as to effect an ever closer union with Him was always the guiding principle of his life.

When reading his life, one can almost hear the Saint addressing the present generation: "Men and women of the twentieth century, endeavor to become human, endeavor to have human thoughts, human feelings, but let these be ennobled and enriched by the divine." The word *human* must not be understood in the sense of not spiritual; one does not cease to be human because he is guided by Christian principles; rather, the human is purified and per-fected.

How wonderful the disposal of Divine Providence! Sanctifying grace, the supernatural life of the soul, does not weaken our natural faculties; the divine and moral virtues do not render the natural virtues superfluous, or lessen their efficacy; on the contrary, they fully develop and perfect them. Nothing of the good, the true, and the beautiful retained after original sin is foreign to the Christian religion; it is presupposed, and Christianity must bring it to its perfection.

Saint Albert clothed his piety in human garb. He was an amiable and sociable Saint. His relations with men were cordial and gained for him the confidence of all who came to him in their difficulties. To his pupils he was ever a friend and brother. As ecclesiastical superior he could reprimand the delinquent and mete out condign punishment, but he never embittered the hearts of his subjects by harshness or severity. He was not of the number of those who believe that sanctity is not compatible with cheerful words and a happy countenance. Singularity and affectation were repugnant to him; his manner was natural and unpretentious; his personality, deeply imbued with grace, made a profound impression on others. His life proves that true Christian piety is attractive, not repelling.

By raising him to her altars, Holy Mother Church does not withdraw him from us; on the contrary, she brings him closer to us. We love him the more, for the aureole of noble manhood encircling his brow has become radiant with the luster of spirituality and grace.

Albertus Magnus, the True Servant of God

By Albertus M. Kaufmann, O.P., S.T.L.

WHEN HOLY MOTHER CHURCH canonizes a saint, she does not simply raise him to the honor of her altars; she points him out to her children as a true servant of God whose life is worthy of imitation. Man's only purpose on earth is to serve God, as the first page of the Catechism teaches; and only they who have fully mastered that important lesson can safely instruct others. Albertus Magnus has been set apart as one of these, and we are admonished to study his life that we may learn to know the real aim and object of living.

In what does the service of God consist? Let Saint Albert himself tell us what he understands by serving God, for his concept of service is the concept of God as it is found expressed in the *Book of Job.* In the first chapter (verses 6-8) we read: "Now, on a certain day when the sons of God (the angels) came to stand before the Lord, Satan also was present among them. And the Lord said to him: 'Whence comest thou?' And he answered and said: 'I have gone round about the earth and walked through it.' And the Lord said to him: 'Hast thou considered my servant Job, that there is none like him in the earth, a simple and upright man, fearing God and avoiding evil?' "

Albertus Magnus in his commentary on the *Book of Job* gives us a beautiful explanation of the words just quoted. He points out that the Lord judges quite differently from Satan concerning Job for the reason that His sentiments are so unlike the sentiments of the evil one. God who is all goodness and love looks with complacency upon the just. Satan, however, is full of hatred and malice toward the good, and he averts his eyes from them out of envy

10

and indignation. The same is true of the sinner, as the Psalmist says (Ps. cxi. 10): "The wicked shall see and shall be angry; he shall gnash with his teeth and pine away" because of envy and rage. Satan refuses to speak about Job; he can report no evil, for he knows none; and he will not say anything in his praise, though he knows all about his good deeds. Now, since Satan is silent, God will commend and glorify his faithful servant. With what love and affection He alludes to him as "my servant," praising his obedience to the law, because in all his works Job declares: "For I am Thy servant and the son of Thy handmaid" (Wis. ix. 5). To help us to understand that Job's obedience is quite extraordinary, God tells us that there is none like to him on the earth. Then, in order that we may know in what Job's holiness and perfection consists, He describes him as a man, simple and prudent—as a man without guile.

He who practices simplicity of intention looks to God alone. His eye, as our divine Savior tells us (Matt. vi. 22), is single and, therefore, his whole body is lightsome. He shuns the duplicity of mind which desires to reign with Christ and at the same time to enjoy the esteem of the world. His virtue, likewise, is simple, arising from a single, unified cause; and it remains unimpaired and uninjured by the diversity of sin. The Apostle well says: "A double-minded man is inconstant in all his ways" (James i. 8). The simplicity of his wisdom is ignorant of subterfuge and cunning in the face of evil.

Job, therefore, well deserves God's commendation as "a man without guile—an upright man, fearing God and avoiding evil." "The just love Thee" we read in the *Canticle of Canticles*. According to Saint Ambrose he is just who makes his will conformable to the will of God; that is, who in every circumstance wishes that God's holy will be done, and that God be thereby glorified. He who is God-fearing is filled with a deep sense of reverence for God and does not only avoid sin itself but also all occa-

11

sions leading to sin. He is always guided by the advice the angel gave to Lot: "Save thy life; look not back, neither stay thou in all the country about; but save thyself in the mountains, lest thou be also consumed" (I. Mos. xix. 17).

Beautiful, indeed, is Saint Albert's portrayal of the true servant of God, but more beautiful still is his own life of service so truly in accordance with the mind and heart of God. In all that he did he was intent on God. The eye of his soul was never dimmed by inordinate self-love. With real generosity of soul he acknowledged himself outstripped by his pupil Thomas, who was to become the Universal Doctor of the Church. In extreme old age, unmindful of his own reputation or the fatigue of a long journey, Saint Albert traveled to Paris to defend the writings of Saint Thomas which were considered by some as too favorable to the unbelieving philosophers. Albert was gifted perhaps more highly than any one of his contemporaries; he possessed a wide knowledge in practically every field of science. His pen was most prolific, and his ability to impart knowledge drew to him thousands eager to hear the words of wisdom coming from his lips. But the esteem of men could not beguile this honest soul into sharing his allegiance between his God and the world.

In the practice of virtue also he preserved an undivided heart. God reigned supreme in his innermost soul; He inspired and directed Albert in every thought, word, and act. Notwithstanding the many vicissitudes of his life, we find no wavering nor indecision, no compromise between right and wrong. "The wisdom of the flesh," as Saint Paul terms it in his letter to the Romans (viii. 6) was unknown to Saint Albert—his was the wisdom of the Holy Spirit; and so well was this fact understood by his fellowmen that they made him arbiter in their differences and disagreements and willingly abided by his decisions.

12

Saint Albert was a just man; he conformed his will always and unhesitatingly to the will of God. The love which directed the will of God directed the will of Albert, and, therefore, he employed his knowledge and spent his energies for the glory of God alone. When devoting himself to worldly matters so contrary to his inclinations, or when in obedience to the Holy Father he accepted the crosier of the bishopric of Ratisbon, he was actuated solely by the desire of promoting the cause of religion and the good of souls. Even in gratifying his longing for undisturbed prayer in his convent chapel, for study, and for writing, he was moved by God's interests. By intimate association with God and constant study of His word and works, Saint Albert learned how good and beautiful, how great and powerful, how wise and loving is the Master for Whom he labored. His service, far from being menial and slavish, was dictated by reverence and filial devotion, and it was this devotion that induced him to guard against sin as an injury and an injustice toward a loving Father. Holy Mother Church places this inspiring portrait before her children and wishes them to imitate it. This applies particularly to all those who, as members of the same illustrious Order, may look upon Saint Albert as their brother in Saint Dominic.

We may not be called to pass our days in the seclusion of a monastery cell; our duties may require an active life in the world—but one thing is common to every vocation; namely, to serve our Maker guilelessly, justly; to fear God and to avoid evil.

Albertus Magnus and the Blessed Sacrament

By Telmus M. Krueger, O.P.

INTENSE LOVE for the Blessed Sacrament was undoubtedly the distinctive feature of Saint Albert's consecration to God. To study and to penetrate the mystic Sacrament in the moments of close union with Christ became the ruling passion of his heart.

His treatise on the Holy Eucharist was not undertaken until he had completed his remarkable explanation of the Holy Sacrifice of the Mass. By constant contemplation of the Holy Sacrament and its strengthening effect in Holy Communion, he immersed himself in the infinite treasures of the Divinity and approached ever closer to Christ, the source of supernatural life and grace. All grace is found in Christ, and of His fullness do we all receive. Saint Albert drew from this treasury the extraordinary strength which enabled him to live interiorly recollected amidst the many distracting duties that constantly harassed him.

Every human heart is filled with unappeased longing for a life of truth and love. This longing like a fiery dart had pierced Albert's innermost soul and caused a thirst which could not be quenched except at the fount of eternal Truth and Love. It urged him to leave home and friends and to journey through Italy and France in search of teachers till finally his languishing soul found rest and refreshment in Him Who says of Himself: "I am the Way, the Truth, and the Life."

Truth and love, the two elements of our supernatural life, the objects of our desires here and of our eternal bliss hereafter, have their beginnings in the soul's union with the Eucharistic Savior. Does not Christ say: "He

14

who eateth my flesh and drinketh my blood hath everlasting life"?

For this reason Albert devoted himself to the contemplation of God, his Lord and Redeemer, in the Holy Sacrament of the Altar. He drew all his extensive knowledge into the service of the work of defining this mystery of mysteries; not, however, in order to completely explain or remove the veil of mystery regarding the real presence under the appearances of bread and wine, but rather to adore on bended knees the marvel of truth and love concealed beneath them.

God enjoins on man the command of adoring His Incarnate Son under the appearances of bread and wine. This injunction aims to counteract man's worst tendency, his pride of intellect. Man desires to create a world emanating from his own mind; but face to face with the mystery of the Eucharist his ambition comes to nought if humility, the handmaid of truth, is wanting to him. Saint Albert, on the contrary, bowed humbly before the humility of his God and was rewarded by a new world opening before him—a world full of grace and truth, flooded with the light of eternal Truth. And in the brightness of this truth he ascended step by step to the very fountain-head of truth, God in the Trinity. There, humbly prostrate in spirit, he asked the gift of this truth, the gift of love and devotion to the eternal Truth, and his prayer was granted.

The human soul aspires with all its powers toward perfection in love, for in every soul there is the desire to hold to the full the eternal substance as a pledge of her share in immortality. The goal of all men is the possession of life eternal in endless love and cognition. We prepare for this state here on earth by the reception of Holy Communion in which Jesus Christ draws us to Himself and makes us members of His Mystical Body. That having been accomplished, our life has reached the zenith of its development; for union with Christ in the Holy Eucharist is the source of the most perfect supernatural love, the love of divine friendship.

Saint Albert found himself constantly drawn to the Heart of Christ in the Holy Eucharist. In the blessed moment of sacramental union he contemplated the abyss of the divine life and divine love in which nonentity reclines upon Infinity and rests close to the Incarnate Deity in order to hear the divine heart-beatings as did Saint John, the beloved disciple.

To belong to God, to constantly renew his consecration to God, to be eternally united with Him—these were the thoughts which surged in Albert's soul as in the ocean of eternal love. But as a true Dominican he desired to share this blessedness with his fellow-men; he desired to sweep them into the fiery current which carries with it everyone who approaches with humility. Thus his love of God set aglow his love of neighbor, and Holy Communion became for him what its name signifies, union in Christ. And in order that this union might be uninterrupted and might embrace all men making them one with Christ, he frequently offered this petition: "Effect, O God, a right faith, a firm hope, and a perfect love in us as Thou didst effect it in all Thy apostles and disciples who received Thy Sacred Body from Thy own hand, so that Thy strength may pour itself forth upon us and bring us to eternal happiness, Thou who livest and reignest with the Father and Holy Ghost through endless ages. Amen."

Albertus Magnus and the Mother of God

By Marianus M. Vetter, O.P., D.D., Ph.D.

I

IN EVERY BIOGRAPHY and in every legend of Saint Albert we find mention of his special devotion to the holy Mother of God. As a youth at Padua it was his custom to kneel in the Dominican church before an image of Mary. Mary was his refuge in trials and cares; she was his counselor in every perplexity. She solved the question of his vocation with the words: "Albert, leave the world and enter the Order of Preachers." A legend relates that to Mary also our Saint is indebted for the extensive knowledge that has gained for him such great renown. Albert, so we read, had great difficulties in his studies and had therefore resolved to discontinue them and to leave the Order. Then the Blessed Mother appeared to him attended by Saint Catherine and Saint Barbara, even as she had appeared to Saint Dominic. Mary consoled her devoted son and urged him to request a favor of her. Albert asked for a comprehensive knowledge of human learning. The holy Virgin granted his petition, promising that no one should surpass or equal him in learning. She assured him, furthermore, of her constant protection against the deceits and snares of the evil one. That he might know, however, that his extraordinary knowledge was the gift of heaven and not a result of his own efforts, she warned him that it would be taken away shortly before his death. As a matter of fact, he completely lost his faculty of memory some time before his death.

Albert's biographers call particular attention to his works on the prerogatives of Mary. Peter of Prussia calls him Mary's private secretary and says that in his praise of

17

Mary, Albert surpassed everything written on that subject. "Jerome, Ambrose, Augustine, Bernard, Anselm, and John Damescene," he writes, "were indeed enthusiastic panegyrists of Mary's dignity and virtues; yet scholarly and sincere as were their encomiums of her greatness, her merit, her power, and goodness, their writings failed to convince the mind and heart as conclusively as did Albert's." Rudolph of Nimwegen writes: "Albert's love for Mary was so great that he could not refrain from her praises. He composed hymns in her honor which he was in the habit of singing on his walks in the garden or during moments of relaxation from work."

Thus we know from legend and from biography that Albert was tenderly devoted to Mary, that Mary pointed out to him his Dominican vocation, and that the extraordinary intellectual achievements that have aroused such great admiration were due to Mary's favor. His was a very personal experience of our heavenly Mother's intercession and powerful influence with her divine Son.

II

Albert's comprehensive work, known as the *Mariale*, is the first evidence we have of his extraordinary love of Mary. Among great minds it is often found that the first production of their pen contains the nucleus of all their future works. This is certainly true of Saint Albert's first work. We find in it deep researches into nature, psychology, and theology. It is remarkable that in his *Mariale* he delineated Mary's physical beauty and made a scientific study even of her complexion, the color of her eyes and hair. It was his deep reverence for the tabernacle of the Incarnate Word which induced him to write in this manner.

With still greater earnestness does the Saint portray the image of the Virgin's soul. He points out that in Mary the natural powers of the human mind reached their highest degree. Then he unfolds the entire realm of the supernatural life and shows that it exists in the soul of Mary in its perfection. In the same manner he explains the three theological virtues of faith, hope, and charity and the four cardinal virtues of justice, prudence, fortitude, and temperance. He interprets likewise the seven gifts of the Holy Ghost: wisdom, understanding, counsel, fortitude, knowledge, piety, and fear of the Lord, and then proceeds to the eight beatitudes and finally to the fruits of the Holy Ghost as described by Saint Paul in his letter to the Galatians (v. 22) : love, joy, peace, patience, meekness, goodness, etc. From this he concludes that all spiritual treasures are hidden in the soul of Mary so that she is truly *gratia plena,* full of grace. He goes even farther and compares her with the angels, describing the characteristic graces of each of the angelic choirs, and proving from Holy Scripture and the teachings of the Church that these same graces adorn the soul of Mary. He undertakes the laborious task of searching among the pages of the Bible for the words of blessing, such as those pronounced on the son of Jacob and others, and then shows that they find perfect fulfillment in Mary. Truly, Mary's image was deeply impressed on Albert's mental vision. Even though we question the legends which have woven themselves about his devotion to Mary, his *Mariale* stands as an incontestable proof of his love for the Mother of God. An echo of this proof is the sermon which he delivered in extreme old age. He had taken as his theme the words in Saint Luke (xi. 27) : "Blessed the womb that bore Thee." He extols her thus: "Oh, how sweet is Mary's image! See, what care artists take to make it surpass in beauty those of other saints. See how solicitous are the faithful to show it due veneration. Churches are adorned with her pictures that our thoughts may dwell devoutly on her. In heaven we shall behold not her image in marble or on canvas, but her own most beautiful soul and body. We shall gaze on her sweet countenance, and its beauty shall ravish us throughout eternity. There we

19

shall approach close to her; there we shall speak to her and not only of her; there we shall be forever inseparably united with her. Oh! when shall the wished-for moment arrive? Do you believe that we shall see her? Do you believe that we shall be permitted to remain always near her? Oh, Mother of mercy, are our names written in the book of life as a pledge that we shall see thee and thy divine Son? Let our tears be our sustenance by day and by night until we shall hear the words: 'Children, behold your Mother! Behold your Brother!' " Thus did a great and learned and saintly man speak with the simplicity of a child when he addressed his Mother in heaven.

III

With a special predilection does Albert explain in his *Mariale* the relation existing between the holy Mother of God and us, her spiritual children. In treating of the virtues, he shows that Mary possessed them in all their perfection: Her maternal love for Jesus, inconceivably great, with which by a special grace she was filled on the day of the Annunciation; the love for us engendered in her heart while offering her divine Son for the redemption of the world; her piety as one of the gifts of the Holy Ghost filling her heart with affection for us, her sinful children, in whom she recognizes the divine image; her mercy toward sinners which we acknowledge as often as we address her as the Mother of mercy. By Mary's intervention sinners are reconciled to God, punishment is averted, graces are obtained, so that she may justly be styled the universal Mediatrix. Mary's relations to us are inexhaustible, as inexhaustible as is Albert's desire to make men fully understand these relations. Thus in his *Mariale* he asks the question: "Is Mary the Mother of all men?" And he answers by showing that Mary has all the prerogatives of motherhood in our regard: a mother bestows life—Mary is the Mother of our life of grace since she gave birth to

Him in Whom we are born anew; a mother fosters life—
Mary in the birth of Jesus provided our every need, temporal as well as spiritual. Her title, Star of the Sea, gives Albert occasion to extol Mary as our guide and protectress on the stormy sea of life; and her title, Gate of Heaven, signifies to him that through Mary comes all created as well as uncreated grace; through her we receive whatever good comes from heaven to earth and ascends from earth to heaven. Albert sums up all Mary's relations to mankind in the simple question: "What does Mary bestow on us out of the fullness of her grace?" He then recounts her gifts: "From Mary do we receive the price of our redemption, the waters of purification, bread for our souls' nourishment, a remedy for our recovery, the armor for our defense, and the reward of merit."

Thus the *Mariale*, Albert's first extensive literary work, gives a comprehensive explanation of the plenitude of grace in Mary, and at the same time testifies to his confidence in her mediation. It is, as it were, the dogmatically scientific basis and the vindication of his veneration for the Mother of God, and he declares that he would feel amply rewarded if by his efforts new clients were brought to the feet of this august Mother.

Another evidence of Albert's eagerness to lead all the world to Mary may be found in a quotation from one of his last sermons: "If a maiden, her arms laden with beautiful flowers, would beckon us to her side, how willingly we would follow the summons; if a queen bade us approach, we would probably do so with some hesitation. But, behold, the Queen of virgins, the Queen of queens calls us, and we heed not her words. Strange inconsistency! The Maiden Mary drew down to earth the Lord of highest Heaven, and now as the Queen of Heaven she is unable to draw us away from this earth so as to make us worthy of Heaven. But let us heed the warning. If in life we disregard the alluring words of the Virgin, it is greatly to

be feared that on judgment day we shall hear the reproach-
ful words of the Virgin's Son."

"It is little, indeed, that Mary requires of her servants.
Mary asks a devoted love and the service of a few short
prayers daily—always on condition, however, that we obey
the commands of her divine Son; for the immediate preparation for the service of the Mother is to be a faithful
servant of her Son, and the immediate preparation for the
service of the Son is to be a faithful servant of His
Mother."

M. V. TESSEN

ALBERTUS MAGNUS
WITH HIS PUPIL ST. THOMAS OF AQUIN

Saint Albert's Consecration
to God in Contemplation
By Hieronymus M. Wilms, O.P., S.T.L.

THE THEOLOGY of Saint Albert, as Doms notes in his excellent commentary on the Saint's teaching regarding Grace, is remarkable for the idea of considering and referring all creation to God in so far as creation finds its perfection in the development and realization of its capacities for good and tendencies toward good by conforming with the ideas existing in the mind of God. Other theologians have written more clearly on the subject of Divine Providence; Saint Thomas more highly extolled the beauty of a soul adorned with virtues, but Albert distinguished himself by his scholarly treatment of the following: the perfection of nature, particularly of human nature; interior development in conformity to the Divine Idea; liberation from the capacity of sinning and from transitoriness; confirmation in grace and, thereby, confirmation in God.

Albert possessed a keen perception and a rare understanding of nature. As a typical Suabian he was endowed with a characteristically Suabian temperament: the changes of seasons, the sight of the fading blossoms of spring put him into a pensive mood. That all things are destined to undergo change; that even the noblest in man is exposed to the danger of perishing; that not only nature is subject to the processes of growth and decay, but that man's earthly life, as well, is controlled by the same forces; that he is born into the world and is subject to continuous change; that he gradually develops to perfect stature, and then sinks down to earth and vanishes from sight; that his activities of knowing and willing, of loving and hating, of committing and omitting are all subject to the same law and follow each other in quick succession—these thoughts moved him deeply.

God, unlike the creatures of His hand, is forever the same in His unity and unchangeableness, and in Him is present the image of man, the clear, unchangeable image of every human being in its perfection as intended by Him. The more clearly Albert saw and understood this, the more deeply did he feel that within himself and round about him all was imperfection and change, and in consequence, the more keenly did he grieve for the causes that brought about this condition. As a first cause he recognized the misuse man makes of his freedom; as a second and more remote cause, original sin; and as a last cause, man's origin—his creation out of nothing. But he saw also God's loving advances through revelation and the means of grace; he saw that through them man might be freed more and more from sin, transitoriness, and change. Here Albert dwells on and develops a thought little noted by other theologians; namely, God's special indwelling in the soul of the baptized. Through the bestowal of sanctifying grace God abides and operates in the soul; and, from the moment the soul arrives at the use of reason, it may comprehend Him by faith, cling to Him by hope, and embrace Him by love, and thus attain firmness and perfection. What use, however, does man make of these divine powers? Doubts and fears harm the persuasion of our faith, and divine truths are but vaguely understood. The hour of meditation in the case of even the most devout is often spent combating distractions; and the will, though splendidly equipped by charity and the other infused virtues, is still weak and vacillating.

When are man's actions entirely good? Even a single deed? All man's works are stamped with the seal of imperfection because all bear the impress of self-love under the ugly form of selfishness which, like the worm in the apple, spoils his noblest actions. Besides, there is a false human respect which is fond of praise and fears blame and criticism. Indeed, can we find a single action of man unmarred by him? And yet it is by our own work that we surrender and dedicate ourselves to God, thus attaining perfection with assimilation to the Divine Idea. This incongruity is aptly expressed in the maxim generally ascribed to Saint Albert: "As often as I have been among men I have returned less a man." He meant to say that whenever he associated with others, even in performing works of charity or mercy, he committed so many faults and imperfections that in the end he doubted whether it would not have been more prudent for him to remain at home and to leave the good work undone. And even if one performs an act, such as expressing a good thought with ardent zeal and true charity exclusively for the good of souls and the greater honor of God, how quickly it passes. It is but a finite act and, moreover, while being performed, excludes every other act. Furthermore, there is, as a rule, reason to doubt whether the work performed was the one willed by God at that moment, or whether he willed another.

Thus Albert saw in all being and action the same change, the same limitation, and the same tendency to sink into nothingness. He realized that this tendency characterizes all being and every human act, even the act of man's self-surrender and dedication to God. This thought took possession of Albert even at the most solemn of such consecrations to God, the holy Sacrifice of the Mass, which, as bishop, he had the privilege of celebrating with all the splendor of a pontifical Mass. During those moments his soul longed ardently for heaven where all change and even the possibility of change would no longer exist; where man is happily deprived of the ability of losing grace; of retracting his consecration to God; of dissolving the bond of Divine union; and of diminishing his ardor of love even for an instant. All these fatal possibilities are incompatible with the glory of eternal bliss, for in this state grace pervades the very substance of the soul, and after the resurrection, the soul in turn pervades the whole body, so that there is no possibility of resisting. The eye of the soul is fixed steadfastly on the resplendent beauty of God, and the will is ardent with the never diminishing glow of purest love, its eternal consecration. Albert examines whether an anticipation of a blessedness at least similar to that of heaven, if not the same, can be attained here below, and joyfully makes an affirmative decision on the question. Time after time he discusses this theme, sometimes calling the *sought-after* a union of love, sometimes contemplation, sometimes affectionate gazing upon God, sometimes adherence to God. He intended these expressions to signify simply a very personal, very consistent giving of one's self to God, closely resembling the state of the Blessed in heaven—in one word, the abandonment to God in actual contemplation.

By contemplation Albert does not understand a state in which the human being lies rigid and motionless, or is raised a few spans above the earth. Such occurrences Albert considered as secondary and quite unessential; neither has he in mind special revelations which may occur even to the sinner; nor has he in mind raptures, such as, according to some theologians, were granted to Saint Paul the Apostle and to Moses, the leader of the Israelites. His idea of contemplation is a loving consciousness of God's presence in the soul by grace, the enjoyment of this possession of God based on faith, love, and the gifts of the Holy Ghost. Albert has described contemplation, perhaps, more clearly than any other writer, as a process of the intellect, for which he does not demand the infusion of intelligible species, but only such images as are man's own acquisition. But by its own effort, the mind is to eliminate from these images all limitation and restriction, so that only the idea of goodness and beauty remains. Into this, the soul immerses itself, borne along by an impulse of love and directed by the Holy Ghost himself. Saint Albert designates the knowledge thus arrived at as tasting of the bourne of love and enkindling new and more ardent love, but distinguish-

26

ing itself completely from any syllogistic deduction of reasoning. Contemplation considered in this sense is to him the most perfect form of self-surrender or consecration to God performable on earth because it excludes more than any other activity the element of change; and because the imperfections of limitation and moral deficiencies are, though not completely, at least to a great extent forced into the background. In this process the human mind is led by the Holy Spirit who causes it to perceive, to see, and to love. In a state of contemplation the element of time so entirely vanishes that a moment may seem like a year; and an hour, like a moment. Man's will surrenders itself to God's will unreservedly because not confined to any condition; it is an assimilation, even a mutual coalescence and blending of all into one. Saint Albert speaks of such a contemplation as being attainable by all who are of good will.

As naturally as Albert had embodied this idea of contemplation in his teachings, so happily did he practice it in his own life. Peter of Prussia tells us that Albert was often seen in contemplation while walking in the convent garden and that all respectfully refrained from disturbing him. His spirit dwelt with God, and the concentration of his thoughts on divine things caused such an intensity of feelings that these betrayed themselves by outbursts into hymns and antiphones. We have a picture by Altheimer of Saint Albert passing his last days in such contemplation. An old man exhausted by the labors of a long active life is seated in his cell, his noble countenance transfigured in prayer. His indefatigable labor in the vineyard of the Lord has consumed all the strength of his body, but his soul is aglow with the freshness of youth uplifted to highest activity in sublime contemplation, in loving, unrestricted abandonment to God.

II

The Secret of Saint Albert's
Dedication of Himself
to Man

Albertus Magnus, the Apostle

By Hieronymus M. Wilms, O.P., S.T.L.

THE PRIME PURPOSE of religious life is the salvation of those who embrace it. The Religious binds himself by the three vows of poverty, chastity, and obedience in order that these vows may protect him against a threefold danger: his vow of poverty overcomes the concupiscence of the eyes; perfect chastity overcomes the concupiscence of the flesh; and humble obedience uproots all pride of life. The Christians of the early ages in order to escape the dangers that surrounded them withdrew from the world and, by preference, spent their lives in the solitude of the deserts. In the beginning they lived as hermits like Saint Paul, their prototype, apart from every other human being; but in later times these men adopted the cenobitic life of Saint Anthony. The cenobites communicated among themselves but had no intercourse whatever with the outside world. An idea of the extent to which this separation was practiced may be gained from the inquiry addressed by one of their number to a visitor as to whether men in the world were still striving for riches, honors, and pleasures. As time went on, these saintly recluses gradually became conscious of the bond of brotherly love existing between them and their fellow men in the world. They became deeply concerned about the eternal welfare of those men exposed to dangers from which their own lives were secure. From that time on a two-fold purpose animated them. They strove not only to save their own souls, but also the souls of their fellow men.

We must not suppose, however, that these religious men exchanged their cell for a life of missionary endeavor. On the contrary, their zeal found expression in prayer and in recommending to God mankind's eternal and temporal welfare.   This apostolate of prayer is well exemplified in the Benedictine Order.   If a monk of Saint Benedict ever engaged in apostolic labor, he did so only in particular circumstances and for a limited period.

The Cistercians, a branch of the Benedictines under a reformed rule, practiced great personal austerities and carried out the idea of vicarious penance.   The monk who throughout life had preserved his soul free from mortal sin must needs have recourse to vicarious penance in order to rouse himself to earnest endeavor during the thirty, fifty, or even seventy years of solitude.   This interior and hidden apostolate took final form and reached its culmination in the Order of Saint Bruno.

The Order of Saint Norbert was the first to engage in an active apostolate, although the sons of Saint Norbert, strictly speaking, are canons regular and not monks.   With the exception of manual labor, the members observed the monastic rule in all its rigor.   For manual labor they substituted labor for souls—preaching and the administration of the sacraments.   In this they were not unlike the parish priest in his ministry, for they brought spiritual aid to the people who settled in the neighborhood of their monasteries.

Saint Dominic went a step further.   As a canon regular of Osma his mode of life was similar to that of the Premonstratensians; but, when the spiritual defection of the faithful in southern France by contact with the Albigensians came to his notice, the resolution formed itself in his mind to found an Order that would not only replace manual labor by study and preaching, but would dispense, moreover, with the *stabilitas loci,* the vow of stability. Dominic did not wish to confine his work to parish ministry; his idea was to organize a band of men free to go wherever the welfare of souls required their services.   Dominic worked strenuously and endured many trials before he accomplished his noble designs and before he obtained the

Papal approbation.   Then, as is usual in the case of great undertakings, a development resulted which apparently surpassed the original intentions of its author.   The founder's conception, though comprehensive and most lofty, was, nevertheless, not all-embracing.   Benedict was perfected by Bernard; Dominic, by Albert; Francis, by Bonaventure.

Dominic well knew that his disciples must be learned men if they were to labor successfully for souls.   For this reason he directed his very first followers to the feet of the learned Roland.   Still, one can hardly maintain that Dominic aimed at anything beyond labor for souls by the preaching of the truth where it was assailed by the heretics or entirely unknown.   But the idea of his Order really comprised more.   The nursery of knowledge and training where the clergy were to be instructed must necessarily be the purest source of truth.   To teach in these schools, to gain influence, to train youth, and thus to teach, as it were, by the mouth of each—all this was comprised in the idea of his Order and was realized as the work progressed. Albert was destined to put the idea into execution, and he finally succeeded in gaining ecclesiastical recognition.

Because the Dominicans studied at the universities and located their houses of study in university cities, they were, as a matter of course, in due time offered chairs in these institutions; for instance, at Paris Albert the Great himself lectured publicly and with such marked success that the largest hall could not hold his audiences.   There had been no official recognition, however, and in the latter half of the thirteenth century violent opposition arose over the disputed right of religious to professorships in the great universities of Europe; mendicants, in particular, were considered ineligible by many.   The struggle lasted through many decades, creating great excitement and suspense throughout western Europe.   Paris, Rome, France, and Italy resounded with the din of verbal onslaughts.   The Pope finally interested himself in the matter and submitted the question to a thorough investigation. He summoned to the Papal court the foremost learned men, Albert the Great being among the number. As instructor during many years at Paris and as organizer of a study plan at Cologne, Albert was thoroughly familiar with the situation of professors and students; moreover, as an earnest religious he was intolerant of anything that would tarnish the grand ideal of the Dominican Order. Albert ranked foremost in this noted gathering, and through the influence that he exerted on all, the question was solved in favor of the Religious Orders. By Papal injunction the work of teaching was designated as compatible to the calling of religious, and official recognition was extended to a practice already in vogue. Opponents were silenced and banished from Paris.

The Order had gained a victory. The joy among Dominican ranks was inexpressible. They were able to realize an ideal that had existed in the mind of their holy Founder; namely, an apostolate of instruction at centers of higher learning. The merit of this accomplishment has sometimes been accorded to Saint Thomas, but not altogether justly. It is established without a doubt that Albert took the lead in these discussions and that the favorable decision was due to his judicious efforts. Albert's work for souls, moreover, as will be noted in the articles that follow, had a wider scope than that of Thomas, although the latter brought to completion the educational system that his master had projected, thereby securing for it such lasting worth.

Albert labored zealously for the welfare of souls, especially among the students of Paris. He not only introduced religious topics in his lectures, but also came into personal contact with his students. They approached him as a father and in all their doubts and difficulties gave him their full confidence. In return he became their counselor and director and formed their souls into the likeness of Him who said: "Learn of Me."

FRA ANGELICO

SAINT ALBERT THE GREAT

Albertus Magnus, the Author

By Hieronymus M. Wilms, O.P., S.T.L.

ALBERTUS MAGNUS departed this life on November 15, 1280, surrendering his body to the earth and yielding his soul into the hands of his Creator. Before his death he bestowed his personal effects as Bishop on the Dominicans at Cologne for the completing of their church; a small sum of money, the disposal of which was granted him by the Holy Father, he donated to an impoverished convent of nuns.

Albertus had died, and yet he lived. His body was not committed to the earth, but was encased in a costly shrine which now rests on the altar of the church of St. Andrew in Cologne. His image continued to live in the memory of the faithful and has remained vivid during the passing centuries. As a fruit of his untiring literary activities he was able to bequeath to posterity a large number of works which, for the most part, were written by himself. In these works Albert's memory has survived to the present day and will survive to the end of time.

The Saint truly fulfilled his Creator's command that man is born to labor—his long life was an uninterrupted succession of study, preaching, instructing, and every other duty that charity or obedience assigned him. Foremost among these activities were his literary pursuits. Many years ago the Reverend Lucas Knackfuss, O.P., produced a series of Dominican pictures. In these he depicted the characteristics of each Saint of the Order. Albertus Magnus is represented as seated at his desk writing. This characterization is well chosen, for there was no period of his life in which he was not thus engaged. He had the habit of writing even on his journeys; as a guest at the convents at which he stopped, he busied himself with his pen, and in departing left the work composed as an expression of his gratitude for the hospitality afforded him.

As a result, his writings at the time of his death were found scattered among the various convents of his Order. Cataloguing, however, was immediately begun. One of these lists dates back to the thirteenth century. In transcribing, the collection was sometimes curtailed and, in some instances, supplemented. Newly found works were added, and spurious ones occasionally found their way into the catalogue.

Great praise is due to the distinguished historian, Dr. Scheeben, for his diligent researches in the past, as well as for his recently instituted thorough investigation of Albert's writings. The list was found to contain 138 works. A negligible number of these are considered of doubtful authorship, so that the minimum number of genuine works may be definitely fixed at 130. The compass of these works naturally varies. Among them are found short treatises; others, again, are so extensive that they might be considered collections rather than single works.

When the art of printing was invented in the fifteenth century, a considerable number of Albert's works came from the press within a short period of time, but no one ventured upon a publication of the collection as a whole, because it was considered too gigantic an undertaking. In 1651, however, the task was accomplished by the Dominican Peter Jammy of Lyons. The edition comprised twenty-one folio volumes and was very nearly complete. In 1890, August Borgnet published thirty-eight imposing volumes at Paris, which as to content are decidedly inferior to the first edition. Since then, other explorers in the field have endeavored to supply the missing parts. Thus we have Dr. Melchior Weiss's critical edition of the *Commentary on Job;* likewise, the Dominican Paul de Loe's critical edition of the *Commentary on Boethius,* and one of Albert's lengthy sermons. Others have given us critically revised

36

editions of Jammy's publication; for instance, Meyer-Jessen's *de Plantis* and Stadler's *de Animalibus*. A new critical edition of the works of Albert as a whole would be most welcome to the many admirers of the Saint.

The writings of Albert the Great may be divided into two large groups: his independent works and his commentaries. It must be noted, however, that when Albert, according to the custom of his times, developed the literary creations of Aristotle or any other writer, he produced works that must be considered distinctly his own, since he employed the originals only in as far as they serve to guide the trend of his thoughts. This holds true even when he simply adds explanatory remarks to the original texts, as he does in his commentary on the works of Aristotle.

Topically Albert's commentaries may be grouped as scientific, mathematical, philosophical, exegetical, and theological. Each one of these categories permits several subdivisions; the philosophical, for instance, may be divided into works on logic, psychology, and metaphysics.

The works of science number not less than thirty-five. The most important among these is his *de Animalibus* which in the estimation of professionals sums up all that the Middle Ages have produced on the subject. Albert did not only delve deeply into primary sources, but he succeeded by means of close observations of his own in supplementing the original, and thus he contributed in not a few instances very valuable information.

Albert's eminent rank among scientists is not based on his discoveries of scientific laws; his distinction is due rather to the fact that he verified by experiment the findings of his predecessors in the field and further developed and enlarged them. Stadler, who is a most competent judge, declared that the author of *de Animalibus* was without a doubt *an observer of the first rank,* whose scientific methods, had they been followed, would have spared scientists the circuitous route of three centuries of investigation. The publishers of his botanical works, Meyer and Jessen, are lavish in their praise of the author. They declare: "He has no predecessor except Theophrast who can compare with him; and of his successors none had so vivid and clear a knowledge of plant nature before the time of Conrad Gessner and Cesalpini. The man, however, who in his own day had so perfect a knowledge of the science, who definitely promoted it, and who during the next three centuries was unsurpassed, certainly deserves the laurels."

Meyer, likewise, does not hesitate to state that during a period of two thousand years there was but one scientific botanist, Albertus Magnus. Wimmer, furthermore, makes the unqualified statement: "Albertus Magnus has studied and described the entire cosmos from stones to stars." Albert's distinctly philosophical writings comprise twenty-three separate works. They make supreme demands on the reader's power of comprehension, for the writer boldly soars to the lofty heights of antiquity's keenest thinker, Aristotle. Up to the time of Albert the Great the Christian world had a more or less antagonistic attitude toward the teachings of Aristotle, because his works were scarcely known except in their Arabian elaboration, and in this form they proved very dangerous to the Faith. Now, Albert's great merit consists in the fact that he discovered the true Aristotle hidden under the false mask; that he revealed him to his contemporaries and thus opened up new realms of philosophy. Professor Grabmann, who was fully acquainted with the source of scientific developments during that period, bestows the highest praise on Albert's achievement, and declares that if he had made no other contribution than this discovery of Aristotle, he would live forever in the history of philosophy. But the Saint also assumed the stupendous task of expounding for the benefit of his contemporaries the complete teachings of the Greek master-mind. These volumes represent a production which is invaluable and which merit the highest encomium;

they prove the close mental kinship between the great German and the greatest of the Greek philosophers.

Among his theological works the Commentary on the Gospel of Saint Luke deserves special mention as the most excellent exegetical production from his pen. Tradition long claimed that this was produced during the years of his episcopacy at Ratisbon; but that opinion was later discredited because the work is so comprehensive and scholarly that, to quote the words of a connoisseur, "If Albert had applied himself to nothing else but the writing of this commentary during his two years at Ratisbon, he would have proved himself a genius in accomplishing the task; and to do so while performing at the same time the ministry of a Bishop would be simply impossible." The excellence of the work may be summed up briefly in these two statements: Albert was familiar with the teachings of the Fathers. He gives an exact and profound interpretation of the text from a theological as well as from an ascetical point of view. The *Summa Theologica* is the most comprehensive and most important of Albert's independent works. In it he endeavored to present in a new, systematic form all the theological learning of the time. This work, like the *Summa* of Thomas Aquinas, unfortunately remained incomplete; it proves, however, the ingenious creative power of an extraordinary man and gives us the opportunity of admiring him, not only at the height, but also at the close of his career; for, when Mary again touched the head of the venerable octogenarian as she had done in his youth, the pen slipped from his trembling hand never to be grasped again. The gifts of knowledge and wisdom, of courage and perserverance which Mary had granted to the earnest student she withdrew from the learned doctor.

We stoop to kiss the pen which was guided by such a hand; and to kiss the hand which labored so unweariedly and so fruitfully, and which by its imperishable productions has erected literary monuments for all future generations.

Albertus Magnus, the Provincial

By Thomas M. Stuhlweissenburg, O.P., S.T.L.

THE ACCOUNT of Albert's election as provincial of the
German province reads as follows: "In 1254 the provincial
chapter was held at Worms; it elected Master Albert, a
highly esteemed instructor, as provincial of the Order in
Germany." The scholarly Dominican fully justified the
confidence his Brethren placed in him when they called him
from the rather restricted activities of lector in a monastery
to the government of a large and extensive province. The
German Dominican province extended at that time from
the English Channel to Poland and from the North Sea as
far south as Austria and Switzerland. It numbered more
than one thousand members in over forty convents.

Albert's activities as provincial were characterized by a
threefold purpose: to expand the Order, to promote the
interior life, and to foster the apostolic spirit among its
members. He founded three convents for men: Strauss-
berg in Thüringen in 1254, Seehausen in Altmark in 1255,
and Rostock in 1256. The foundation of the Dominican
convent for women at Paradies (Paradise) near Soest was
brought to completion during his term of office, and in
1255 he received the vows of the first twelve Sisters.

On his visitations to the conventual houses he left salu-
tary precepts formulated at the annual provincial chapters
for the promotion of piety and an earnest religious spirit.
Albert's zeal was especially directed toward the faithful
and conscientious practice of holy poverty; he desired to
see his Brethren live as mendicants and to possess abso-
lutely nothing. At a provincial chapter held at Worms at
which he presided the resolution was taken to exhume the
body of a Brother and bury it in unconsecrated ground.
Clothing and money held without the knowledge of his

40

Superior had been found among the Brother's effects at the time of his death.

Another regulation drawn up at the same chapter forbade the Brethren to make use of a conveyance or to ride on horseback when travelling, and prescribed fasting and discipline as penance for any infraction in this matter. Albert forbade that exemptions from this rule be granted to anyone. Thus, he assigned to the Prior of Krems a seven days' fast, five recitations of the Penitential Psalms and as many disciplines because he had made use of a conveyance while on a journey. The Prior of Minden was penanced with three disciplines, three recitations of the Penitential Psalms, and five days of fasting for making the journey to the chapter on horseback.

In a special circular the Saint informed the members of his province regarding his conception of the vow of poverty and added definite injunctions. His life was in perfect accord with his teaching and served as a powerful incentive to his subjects in the practice of the holy vow of poverty. He made all his journeyings on foot and without money, depending on alms for subsistence. He desired to live in poverty with his Brethren even as Christ had lived with his Apostles, in order that his Order, which was founded for the salvation of men, might carry out the apostolate of Christ.

By his encouragement and his exertions, apostolic activities spread into parts of Europe still under the influence of pagan customs. In 1256 he appealed to the priors and Brethren of the province to extend their labors to missionary lands. The Saint's zeal, however, was not restricted to his provincial duties. Cologne requested him to act as mediator in its difficulties with Bishop Conrad of Hochstaden. Albert succeeded in bringing about a peaceful settlement and earned for himself the undying gratitude of the citizens of Cologne. In 1256 the Pope summoned Albert to Anagni, the seat of the Papacy at the time. The

University of Paris and the Mendicants were engaged in a violent struggle. The very continuance of the two Orders was in question. The Saint defended the cause of the Mendicants so ably and so convincingly that the Pope decided in favor of the Orders. At this time the Pope detained Albert at the court where the latter was obliged to conduct a course of lectures in theology.

Four years only did this great man serve his Order as provincial. "On account of his matchless knowledge he was released from the office of provincial by the general chapter of Florence in 1257." The Order wished to give back to science, this, its most erudite and distinguished Master.

Albertus Magnus, Bishop of Ratisbon
By Polycarp M. Siemer, O.P., Ph.D.

BEFORE engaging in an important undertaking, a prudent man will give his project forethought and will deliberate how best to realize his objective; he will consider whether he is physically and mentally fit for assuming the responsibilities accompanying the enterprise. Above all, he will reflect if he may rightly expect the help of God in the venture he is about to make. The novice desiring to dedicate himself to God by the vows of religion considers long and seriously the obligations of his new state of life; and the young man who aspires to the priesthood passes many years in preparation for the day on which the Bishop will place consecrating hands upon him.

An event of the greatest significance in the life of our Saint was his appointment by Alexander IV in 1260 to the vacant see of Ratisbon. Albert had hitherto lived the apostolic life of a Dominican, garbed in the black and white habit of the Order. Animated like his holy founder by a great love for Christ and an earnest desire to lead souls to Him, he had penetrated deeply the mysteries of nature and grace, of human learning and Christian faith. Year after year he had generously dispensed the treasures of the natural sciences and supernatural truths to his fellowmen. He had been active as lector and preacher in the German convents at Hildesheim, Freiburg, Ratisbon, and Strassburg; as instructor at the universities of Paris and Cologne; as provincial of the Order in Germany; and as arbiter for peace between the city of Cologne and Archbishop Conrad of Hochstaden.

This intensively apostolic career was suddenly interrupted when the Pope's choice of a bishop for Ratisbon fell upon Albert. Alexander IV entreated him to accept the office,

43

but Albert refused. Did he on account of his advanced years consider himself physically and mentally unfit to bear the onerous burden? The retiring Bishop of Ratisbon had mismanaged the temporal as well as the spiritual affairs of the diocese, and conditions were consequently most deplorable.

We know that the Master General, Humbert, addressed a most impassioned letter to Albert praying and conjuring him to decline the honor of the episcopacy and to persevere in the poor and humble life of a Dominican friar. What could have been more to the liking of a true son of the apostolic Dominic, such as we know our Saint to have been? But the Pope's only reply to Albert's protestations was the express command to accept the appointment and with the grace of God to effect the reform of the diocese. The will of God had thus manifested itself, and Albert yielded. He was anointed with the holy chrism, and assumed, together with the exalted dignity of the episcopacy, the difficult task of governing one of the largest dioceses of Germany.

It must have been a singular surprise to the clergy and people of Ratisbon to learn early one morning that the new Bishop, attended by a few of his Brethren, had quietly arrived the previous evening after sunset and was to be formally installed in the diocese that day. It was customary for princes of the Church in those days to enter their sees amid ecclesiastical pageantry; Albert's manner, therefore, pointed to a turn in affairs. In fact, Albert had come as a reformer authorized by Christ's representative, and he was determined to raise the religious and the moral life to a higher plane and to retrieve the temporal welfare of his diocese. But what could be more effective in bringing about a reform among the clergy and laity than the exemplary life of its supreme pastor, his apostolic mode of living, his unimpeachable, edifying conduct? Albert, as leader of men, recognized the importance of this procedure. As

Bishop he continued to live the life of a Dominican friar. His biographers tell us that when he put off the friar's garb, he retained the friar's mode of life.

Animated with a truly apostolic spirit, Albert set to work with characteristic prudence, vigor, and determination. His chief concern was the spiritual welfare of the souls entrusted to him. Convinced that a renewal of spirit among the clergy was the only effective way of bringing about a reform among the laity, he began his visitation of the clergy, of parishes, and of convents. Convents as centers of exemplary Christian living proved powerful factors in the reform he so successfully achieved. He made his journeys for the most part on foot shod with the coarse boots in use among the Friar Preachers, from which circumstance the nickname "Boots, the Bishop" was sportively coined.

What happiness was his when on his apostolic journeys he had the opportunity to pass a few days under the peaceful roof of a convent! He devoted these leisure hours to contemplation on the writings of the Fathers, and as a fruit of his studies he left to the religious a written treatise on the subject when departing. As a result of this practice Albert's Commentary on the Gospel of Saint Luke was produced, a work which testifies to the Bishop's correct conception of the evils of his day, and which in the words of one of his biographers proves him to be a second Saint Luke—a physician and a healer of men's souls. He encouraged his clergy by word and example to lead pious and pure lives. Mindful of his vocation as a Friar Preacher he taught the word of God to the people on his visitation tours. He stressed the great value of divine services, especially the holy sacrifice of the Mass as the central mystery of the Christian faith. He pontificated in his cathedral on every feast celebrated by the Church.

On these occasions, attended by his cathedral chapter, he wore all the insignia of his episcopal office, deeming only the most splendid regalia worthy of God's service and conducive to His greater glory. Thus the blessing of God was not wanting to his undertakings. Soon a religious revival, which was readily followed by a revival of morals, took place among clergy and people. Albert, moreover, induced the neighboring Bishops to introduce reformatory measures in their dioceses, thus extending his sphere of action and exercising a saving influence on numerous souls outside the fold entrusted to his care.

The great Bishop considered it his duty, furthermore, to improve the shattered financial conditions of his diocese. An old chronicler describes the affairs in these words: "Albert found the treasury empty, the casks drained, the granaries bare." To make matters worse, the diocese was heavily in debt. Would the learned and apostolic Bishop be able to contend with these difficulties? Would he prove himself a practical businessman? Albert set about the task with his usual wisdom and energy. He ordered that all episcopal estates, fields, and vineyards be put under cultivation, that all revenues be carefully administered, that the strictest economy be observed in his household, and that stern regulations be enacted against all who in any manner defrauded the Church of her property. Consequently he succeeded in defraying in a short time an encumbering debt, and establishing order where he had found financial chaos. The chroniclers of Ratisbon speak with admiration of this reform so quickly accomplished.

Albert's system of economy did not, however, prevent him from giving generously to the needy, sick, and helpless. In the spirit of evangelical charity he aided impoverished members of his cathedral chapter and sent alms to many convents, especially if the latter in turn practiced charity toward the destitute. With what spirit he was animated may be seen from a circular addressed to the diocesan clergy: "We must anticipate the final harvest by works of mercy and, looking forward to the eternal riches, sow in time what hereafter we shall bountifully reap. In doing this we must be inspired by a firm hope and great confidence: 'he who soweth sparingly shall reap sparingly; but he who soweth in blessings shall also reap blessings' and shall merit eternal life." Do not these words prove the apostle of charity, the true follower of the Master whose new commandment is the commandment of charity?

Like Saint Thomas, Saint Albert possessed the characteristic trait of directing all his energies toward one objective, to gain souls for Christ. His diligent scientific researches and his profound learning did not estrange him from his fellow-men; they presented to him all things in their true nature and in their correct relationship to each other. Does not this fact account for his singular business ability? And must not his conquest of souls and the revival of religious and moral life among priests and laity be attributed to his ardent love for Christ and to his sincere piety and exemplary apostolic manner of life?

Albertus Magnus stands before us as one of the greatest German bishops whose achievements during the two short years of his episcopate are amazing. His resignation after two years and his return to his convent are eloquent proofs of his ever-increasing leaning toward contemplation, of his self-effacing spirit, and especially of his love and fidelity to his Order.

Albertus Magnus, the Preacher

By Meinrad M. Schumpp, O.P., S.T.M.

CHRIST'S last commission to His apostles was an authoritative command to preach the gospel throughout the world. They were to make His doctrine known to all men and to baptize them in the name of the Most Holy Trinity. Carrying out this command and fulfilling it to the best of their ability, they finally sealed their ministry with their life's blood. Saint Paul writing to the Corinthians was animated with the same spirit: "If I preach the gospel, it is no glory to me, for a necessity lieth upon me: for woe is unto me if I preach not the gospel."

Saint Dominic, who had ever vividly before his mind the ideal of a perfect life based upon the teachings of Christ, had no other view in calling into being the Order of Friar Preachers than that which inspired the labors of his patron, the great apostle of the Gentiles. His spiritual sons were to aid in executing Christ's commission to spread His kingdom on earth; they were to say with the apostle: "The preaching of the gospel lieth as a necessity upon me: woe to me if I preach not the gospel."

Do we perceive this same apostolic zeal urging Albert to preach the gospel? Did he render important service in the pulpit as well as in the lecture hall? The Saint's renown is founded principally upon his scientific contributions, which were simply a method to him of making known the mercies of God to all the world. But over and above this assiduous labor, the fruitfulness and importance of which can hardly be overestimated, Albertus Magnus, like a true Friar Preacher, occupied himself in lovingly breaking the bread of life to the illiterate and lowly. The earliest biographers omit not to refer to Albert's zeal in preaching the word of God to the people. Henry of Herford relates: "He prayed with great fervor, preached the word of God from

48

time to time, and gave wholesome counsel to all who requested it. By his gentle and persuasive manner he exerted an astonishing influence upon souls." In the so-called "Legend of Cologne" he is mentioned as a *distinguished preacher,* and manuscripts of the Middle Ages call him simply *Preacher-Bishop.* If his merits in this field had not been so universally recognized, Pope Urban IV would not have appointed him preacher of the Crusade to all German-speaking lands. Although at this time nearly seventy years old, Albert complied and devoted himself to the enterprise with youthful energy. He continued a *Friar-Preacher* and *Preacher-Bishop* to the end.

Our Saint was not, however, so powerful and eloquent a speaker as Bertold of Ratisbon, his contemporary; nor was his pulpit like that of the latter surrounded by thousands, so that the churches could not contain the audiences; his words were simpler, plainer, calmer as is proper for a man of learning. Yet his influence as a preacher is not diminished by this circumstance, especially at a time when preachers were few. This accounts for the fact that the memory of the great *Preacher-Bishop* and his fruitful ministry lasted and was made the background for many a beautiful legend associated with his name. A heretic, so the people of Ratisbon related several centuries later, who had dared to mount the pulpit once occupied by the Saint, was instantly struck dumb. Not until he had ascended another pulpit did he regain the power of speech.

It was common for monasteries in that day to train their members assiduously in the art of preaching. There were numerous methods of procedure in circulation, and we need not be surprised to find one such, both in old print and manuscript, attributed to the renowned Master. Many a word supposed to have been spoken by the learned Preacher traveled from mouth to mouth and not seldom assumed a written form. We find recorded that Brother Bertold of Ratisbon, country preacher, called on Albert to receive instructions from him. One of the questions asked was the following: "What Christian work is most pleasing to God?" Albert replied: "If one sees his fellow-man in great labor and distress and consoles him by word and work and assists him as much as possible, that, before God, is the most pleasing work a man can perform." An answer truly worthy of so untiring a laborer in the vineyard of the Master!

Various collections of sermons bearing his name are extant: on the *Valiant Woman* in the *Book of Proverbs;* on the *Sunday Gospels;* on the *Holy Eucharist;* on the *Blessed Mother.* Not all of these enjoy an undisputed claim to authenticity; furthermore, a great number of them are not exact transcripts, but only Latin sketches serving as outlines for sermons delivered in the German tongue. Many bear throughout the imprint of the age in their tendency to adhere strictly to a *schema,* as do the sermons of Saint Bonaventure; they betoken that moral earnestness and straightforwardness which characterize all of Albert's works. Frequently we hear him lash the evils of society: intemperance, a passion for gambling, desecration of the Lord's Day, injustice. He spares neither the great nor the lowly; the young nor the old; bishops nor secular princes.

When the great bishop and preacher, Melchior of Diepenbrock, calls the printed sermon "the living breath transformed into an ice-blossom on the cold window pane," we may apply it in a superlative degree to the transcripts of the Saint's sermons which are at best very meager sketches and which give us a very imperfect idea of the profound impression produced by a personality at once so ingenious and so saintly as that of Albertus Magnus.

It is the teaching of Saint Thomas that in heaven teachers and preachers are adorned with a special aureole and enjoy a special beatitude. If our gaze at present rests upon our Saint in the blessedness of heaven, then it is fitting that we be reminded that one jewel in the celestial diadem is reserved for the *Friar-Preacher* and *Preacher-Bishop.*

Albertus Magnus, the Peacemaker

By Guenther M. Ruppert, O.P.

CHILDREN of Saint Dominic! Peacemakers! How close the relationship between these terms! Saint Catherine of Siena adorned with the palm of peace has scarcely passed from before our admiring gaze when a great German personage rises before our mental vision. His eyes beam forth love and his hands bespeak kindness. It is Albertus Magnus. Peace was to him a delightful companion along life's journey.

Among the learned of his day Albert's place is uncontested. The Church has justly entitled him *Doctor Universalis.* The centuries have but added to the luster of his name. He was a leader in every field of scientific endeavor. We recall his services to the Church as preacher, papal-delegate, bishop, professor, and pastor of souls; likewise, his benevolent and social activities. In the turmoil of the thirteenth century which inaugurated a general re-evaluation of things, Albert, the simple mendicant friar, gains glorious distinction for himself as a diplomat. His biographers refer to him as the peacemaker. Could nobler title be conferred on mortal man? The loftiest aspirations of the nations are aspirations for peace.

Albertus Magnus was intensely interested in the political life of the city of Cologne, and it is not surprising that its citizens hold him still in grateful memory. The social virtue of justice which he possessed in so marked a degree fitted him admirably for the work Divine Providence had destined for him. In those days, as well as today, men's passions had to be reckoned with in politics. Nations, however, lived by Faith: one God, one ruler. They readily submitted to the leaders who announced peace in Christ's name.

51

In 1250 Archbishop Conrad of Hochstaden and the citizens of Cologne were engaged in bitter strife. The merchants, arrogant in their wealth and power, refused to recognize the rights of the Archbishop and determined to totally emancipate themselves from episcopal jurisdiction. The Archbishop, a quarrelsome man, resolved in turn to humiliate and penalize the citizens. He levied a heavy toll on all merchandise, which heretofore had been exempted from dues. Without the slightest regard to the municipal privilege of free mintage, he coined his own money whenever he pleased. To a complaint on the part of the citizens he responded by a challenge to arms, and in 1251 his troops besieged the city. The siege proved a failure, and after some delay an armistice was concluded. Two Dominicans, the cardinal-legate, Hugo of Saint Sabina and Brother Albert, lector of the Friar Preachers in Cologne, were appointed to arbitrate in the matter. Since Hugo was travelling at the time, Albert rendered the decision alone which, however, with a few alterations, was approved by the legate on his return in 1252. The contract testifies clearly to the Saint's wisdom and to his keen sense of justice. The Archbishop was permitted two coinings of good impressions; merchandise was declared exempt from duty, but the citizens on their part had to promise under oath not to import goods in their own name in order to render them immune from taxes. Finally a general amnesty was to go into effect. Smuggling, tax-evading, amnesty—what familiar terms!

Human passions soon made void the peace pact. While Albert was absent in Italy in 1256, the Archbishop, in requital for an attack upon a canon, again began hostilities, and a bloody encounter ensued near the village of Frechen, in which Conrad was beaten. Again there were peace negotiations, and again Albert came forward as arbiter. He carefully weighed demands and counter demands; he established correct relations between claims and charges and adjusted matters so that grievances were allayed. But for a

52

second time the results were of short duration, and both parties resumed the conflict. Albert, however, stands out all the more resplendent, because of so dismal a background. He ranked high above both parties because he strove for truth and justice, not for personal aggrandizement or profit. He labored perseveringly to reconcile those estranged, and in this manner laid a stable foundation for the luxurious growth of his city of Cologne. In 1492 Albert's first biographer, Kölhof, a citizen of Cologne, concluded Rudolf of Nimwegen's *Legenda Literalis de Alberto Magno* with the significant words: "Blessed art thou, city of Cologne, because thou didst possess Albert who by his eloquence arrested bloodshed and rebellion."

It was during this period of turmoil and confusion in the city-states that the bitter contest existing between the University of Paris and the Mendicant Orders was most vehement. Rudolf remarks that the enemies were so merciless that, had not the pious King Louis and his brother Alphonse befriended the Order, it would have been destroyed. The Dominicans submitted the affair to Alexander IV at his court in Anagni. Albert stated the case and refuted the charges with such keenness of mind, clearness of insight, and holy eloquence that he won a complete victory over his antagonists. Chief among these was William of Saint Amour, whose treatise, *The Perils of These Latter Times,*—a work maliciously attacking the Friars and particularly the Dominicans—was formally condemned by the Pope. Though Albert took a firm stand in exposing and disproving the false charges of the opponents, he did not wound charity, as is proved by the many reconciliations made soon after.

Frankish documents attest that during the years of his sojourn at Würzburg, Albert acted in the capacity of peacemaker and as such his name is attached as witness to important public documents. On December 4, 1264, he effected a peaceful settlement between the collegiate church of Saint John of Haug and the nobleman, Gottfried of Hohen-

lohe, regarding the respective rights of the provost of
Hopferstadt and Rudershausen. The following year he in-
tervened in the quarrel of the above-mentioned Church of
Saint John and Bishop Iring of Würzburg respecting the
rights of the provost and the Councils of Königshofen,
Wolkshausen, Eichelsee, and Heochsheim. His judgment
was also sought in purely worldly matters. Thus on July
1, 1265, he arbitrated in the case of Wegenheim at Würzburg who had erected stables so close to the custom house
that they interfered with the lighting of the building. Albert
was, likewise, a member of the committee to which was
entrusted the difficult adjustment of the juridical and mili-
tary affairs between Bishop Iring and the city of Würzburg.
The public records of the year 1267 show that he was in-
strumental in a successful peace-negotiation between the
Brother Hospitalers of Saint John in Würzburg and the
knight Marquard. Many other instances might be cited of
conciliations promoted by the Saint, but the few that have
been mentioned prove adequately that in addition to scientific research, strenuous teaching and preaching, he accomplished a multiplicity of tasks unavoidable in an age torn by
the disorders of petty wars and rendered difficult because
complicated by the diversity of local laws and statutes.

Albert returned to Cologne in 1271. New difficulties had
arisen in his absence between Archbishop Engelbert and
the citizens. Regardless of the sacredness of his person,
Count William of Jülich had held Engelbert imprisoned in
the castle of Nideggen during a period of three years. The
count was excommunicated, and the city placed under interdict. Albert's arrival filled all hearts with courage and hope;
for they knew he was the bearer of peace. In the *Apologia*
of the Archbishopric of Cologne we read: "In the year 1270,
by the kind intervention of the Bishop of Ratisbon (Albert)
the papal interdict was removed with the provision that the
citizens recognize the archbishop as their lord and perform
what is of obligation to them (which they have sworn to

do) ; and that the archbishop will not revenge himself upon the count nor upon the city, but that as a father he will suffer the insult to be forgotten."

And now the time for rest was approaching for the aged bishop. He spent the remaining years in the Convent of Holy Cross at Cologne devoting himself to teaching and writing. However, in 1274, he left the solitude of the cloister to be present at the Council of Lyons. He was energetic in promoting the election of Rudolph of Hapsburg as king of Germany, thus aiding to bring the *Interregnum* to an end, that period which had been so productive of disorder, unrest, and bloody strife.

For the last time we see Albert making a journey to Paris on foot. With energetic and holy zeal the venerable old man upholds the work of his renowned pupil, Saint Thomas. Then at last comes to him the peace of Christ in the kingdom of Christ. Albertus Magnus died a holy death at the age of eighty-seven years.

III
Supplement

Veneration and Canonization of Blessed Albertus Magnus

By Robert M. Klostermann, O.P., Ph.D., S.T.L.

LOFTY ideals and strength of character are the chief quali-
ties indicative of a really great personality. The more deter-
minedly a man strives toward noble ideals, the more he will
perfect himself and the more he will contribute to the true
welfare of his fellowmen for all times. We find this law
verified in the instance of all great characters in the past.
Time has proved that great men never appear singly in history; they are always closely associated with kindred spirits
who labor zealously and perseveringly for the realization of
their leader's ideals. Indeed, the first enthusiastic followers
often win the recognition of the world long before the master himself gains renown. The life of Saint Albertus Magnus bears out this statement. His pupil, Thomas of Aquin,
was raised to the Altars of the Church many centuries
before a like honor was accorded Saint Albert.

Today Albert is recognized by Holy Mother Church and
her faithful children as one of God's saints. A glance over
the past will reveal the earnest and persevering effort required on the part of men of learning as well as of the
German people to make possible the canonization of their
renowned countryman.

Albert's veneration among the faithful had a gradual
development. A short time after his death, Lauingen, the
place of his birth, dedicated a memorial chapel to him. At
his tomb in the Dominican convent at Cologne, bands of
pilgrims offered their prayers and implored their patron's
intercession with God in their trials and sufferings. The
faithful saw in him from the beginning, not only a great
and learned man, but also a friend of God who was plead-

ing their cause in the heavenly realms. The University of Cologne gave a powerful impetus to the Saint's cause in the fifteenth century by requesting the exhumation of his body. The great number of miracles in response to the prayers of the faithful finally induced Innocent VIII to allow the erection of altars in his honor and the celebration of his feast in the churches of Cologne and Ratisbon. Some time later the feast was extended to the whole Order. In Cologne it was no longer celebrated on November 1, as formerly, but on the day of his death, November 15. In the church of Saint Andrew—the old Dominican church had been destroyed—a new altar was dedicated to him and his relics enshrined therein. Although his veneration continued to spread, it failed to bring about his formal canonization. New difficulties constantly frustrated the earnest desires of his devoted clients. These difficulties, however, were of a purely political and economic nature and bore no relation whatever to Albert's private or public life.

At the Vatican Council the German bishops addressed a petition to Pius IX urging him to decree to Albert the glory of a Doctor of the Church. Their request remained unanswered at the time; nevertheless, a keen interest in the cause and in the life of the great man was aroused. They endeavored to prove scientifically that Albert held a prominent rank among the learned of the Middle Ages and that he was not even overshadowed by Thomas of Aquin. This new enthusiasm caused petition after petition to be sent to Rome. The Academic League and the German bishops united in behalf of the entire Catholic world, and German Catholics had the good fortune to find in Cardinal Frühwirth, O.P., an enthusiastic and untiring advocate in the promotion of their cause. The aged cardinal, moreover, was ably assisted in his endeavors by two learned Germans, Dr. Angelus Walz, O.P., in Rome and Dr. Scheeben in Cologne. After much prayerful deliberation and a careful examination of the cause, Pope Pius XI on December 16,

1931, finally accorded to Albert the full honors of the altar, as well as the glory of a Doctor of the Church.

It was an hour of supreme happiness especially for the German people when their great Albert was proclaimed a Saint by Holy Mother Church. Let us hear the Holy Father's own words: " ... Therefore, We entrusted the whole matter to the Sacred Congregation of Rites. Our dear sons, the Cardinals of the Sacred Congregation, met in assembly on December 15 to hear the report of Our well-beloved son, Francis Cardinal Ehrle, the Promoter of the Cause. An official historical investigation had previously been made regarding the holiness of Blessed Albert's life as well as the lawfulness of the religious veneration given him; furthermore, two learned men officially appointed and thoroughly qualified had given a verdict in writing regarding his teaching. After taking the votes of the official prelates of the same congregation of Rites, and all these reports having been duly considered and discussed, the members of the assembly unanimously agreed that We be requested to grant the favor. Therefore, on the following day—that is, today—Our beloved son, Salvator Natucci, having given a careful report of all these matters, We fully concurred and most willingly approved the decision of the Sacred Congregation.

"Therefore, in virtue of Our Apostolic Authority, We ordain that the feast of Saint Albert the Great with the rank of a minor double, with the Office and the Mass of Confessor and Pontiff, with the addition of the title of Doctor be celebrated each year by the Universal Church on November 15.

"Let thanksgiving be offered to God Who in the wonderful designs of His providence has deigned through Us His servant to perfect the glory of Albert the Great in the Church Militant. Divine Providence has revealed Saint Albert in our age as a shining light which, like the rising

61

sun, illuminates and gives fecundity to the entire organism of the Church, 'laboring not for himself alone, but for all who seek the truth.'

"May Saint Albert the Great, then, be our intercessor—he who from earliest youth strove after wisdom and virtue and bore the Lord's yoke cheerfully even as Saint Paul the Apostle, who thought nothing could be more desirable than to bring into captivity every understanding unto the obedience of Christ."